WAVES OF GOODBYE

A Story of Pet Loss & Comfort

By Kristen Halverson
Illustrated by Tatiana Kutsachenko

Second Edition
Hardcover: ISBN-9781087945675
Library of Congress Control Number: 2021901385
Cover Art and Interior Illustrations by Tatiana Kutsachenko
Book Layout by Indie Publishing Group, Inc.
Photo of Sunrise and Ocean Waves by Raimond Klavins on Unsplash

Publisher:
Kristen Halverson
14104 225th Street
Elkader, Iowa 52043

Visit author and publisher website at www.kristenhalversonbooks.com

Printed in the United States of America

Disclaimer: The content of this juvenile fiction book provides some basic information about handling pet loss.
This book is not intended as a substitute for treatment and/or consultation with a licensed practitioner, who treats the management of grief.

In loving memory of Emma Rose and Ella Rose, who both blessed me with their beautiful souls.

For Frances Cates, who serves as an angel to many in their waves of goodbye.

As the fall leaves fell upon the running river, I was losing my best friend, Emma Rose. She had been sick for a long time.

Sadly, it was time for us to say goodbye. I gave Emma Rose one last warm nuzzle as I felt her go into the cool autumn wind.

As Emma Rose left me, tears ran down my whiskers. Losing an animal friend is awfully hard. My sad feelings rocked me like ocean waves.

The loss of Emma Rose broke my heart. We were playmates and best friends. Most of all, she was always there to comfort me. We spent every moment together.

Later that night, as I stared at the stary night sky, I had several questions about the passing of my best friend.

Why did she have to leave me? Was she still suffering? What was she doing now? Did Emma Rose miss me?

I sure missed her. I felt lost without her.

As the moon shone upon me, I cried myself to sleep. I dreamt of an elephant, a tabby cat, and a fluffy dog walking on a beautiful beach. The elephant gently placed her trunk on my heart.

She whispered, "You're going to be alright. I know your heart is breaking. My name is Ella and these are my friends, Winter and Milagro. We're here to comfort you during your time of loss."

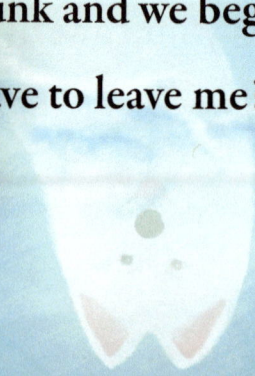

Ella lifted me up with her long trunk and we began to walk along the beach.

I asked, "Why did Emma Rose have to leave me?"

Ella replied, "Emma Rose was an older dog who lived a beautiful long life. But she'd been ill for some time. Our furry friend's time on this earth is short, as their life span isn't as long as our human friend's. Emma Rose shared a wonderful life with you. The grief you feel is normal and natural. Feeling sad is the biggest expression of your love for her."

Winter, the striped cat, placed her paw upon mine.

She meowed, "Crying is part of expressing your sadness. Everyone shows their grief in different ways. I know you feel like you're crying waves of goodbye tears, but they won't last forever."

I asked, "Is Emma Rose still sick?"

Winter replied, "Emma Rose is with her other animal friends. She's playing with them and feeling young again. Emma Rose is no longer suffering."

As the sun began to rise, Ella wiped more tears from my face.

She said, "You're going to be alright, I know your heart is filled with an ocean of tears right now. It helps to share your loss with your family and friends."

Ella's calm voice comforted me as I gazed at the rolling sea, but my heart still ached.

Soon, Winter called me to the water's edge.

She meowed, "See how the ocean waves come and go? This is how loss feels. While you're grieving the loss of Emma Rose, you may feel upset, confused or even sad. These feelings will come and go."

I meowed, "Winter, I'm afraid to share my feelings with others."

Winter purred, "As Ella said, sharing your loss with others will comfort you. Remember, your friends and family have experienced loss too. They'll understand your feelings and want to help you."

Ella picked me up with her strong trunk and we strolled a little while longer. Once again, she dried my tears.

She said, "When we lose our animal friends, it allows us to learn how to let go. It also teaches us how to overcome other struggles that we may endure in our life journey. One day, you may lose another animal friend. This experience will make you stronger."

I asked my new friends, "Where's Emma Rose now? Will I ever see her again?"

Ella whispered, "Emma Rose is in the most heavenly place filled with love. Yes, you will see her again. Emma Rose is waiting for you and misses you too. She understands that your heart is hurting. Emma Rose wants you to live your best life. She will live in your heart forever, and she will always be with you."

Suddenly, we heard Milagro barking. Ella, Winter, and I walked over to see what he wanted to show us.

Milagro was drawing a picture of Emma Rose's face in the sand with his paw.

He said, "You could make an Emma Rose photo album to celebrate her life, or do something good for the community in her memory. For example, when my cat friend, Masha, passed, I donated to the Meow Village Cat Rescue. Now, my donation will help other cats in Masha's name."

As tears ran down my face, I touched Milagro's paw and purred, "Thank you. That's a great idea. It also makes me feel a little better."

Milagro barked, "Come with me! I have something special to show you."

In an instant, I saw a beautiful rainbow floating over the ocean.

He whispered, "Your sadness will only last for a moment in time. Emma Rose will live in your heart every day. You'll feel the waves of grief splashing against you in the coming days or even months, but a rainbow will soon appear in your life. Thinking about the good times you shared with Emma Rose will bring joy to your heart."

Ella picked me up one last time and placed her trunk on my heart.

She whispered, "Losing an animal friend makes our hearts hurt and ache. You'll get through this difficult and sad time. Remember the wisdom we shared. It will bring comfort to you as you go through the waves of goodbye."

I meowed, "I still feel so lost without my best friend."

Ella replied, "Feeling lost without Emma Rose by your side is normal. Again, sharing your feelings with your friends and family will help you. I want you to celebrate Emma Rose's life with others. Tell them what a terrific friend she was through a poem, a painting, a letter, or even a book."

I meowed, "I do love art. I'll make a pretty painting of Emma Rose to share with my friends."

Winter purred, "Look at the sunrise! You'll feel the sun's warmth again after your time of grief passes."

Then Milagro whispered, "Emma Rose loves you and doesn't want you to be sad for too long. She wants you to give and share love with your other animal friends. I believe Emma Rose is waiting for you beyond the sun where the waves of goodbye end."

Before Ella walked away, she said, "I want you to know that you're never alone in your sadness."

After we said goodbye, Ella, Milagro, and Winter faded away into the sunrise.

When I woke up from my dream, I felt the warm morning sun upon my face. As I looked up at the beautiful sky, I saw a special heart-shaped cloud. I knew it was a sign from Emma Rose to reassure me that the waves of goodbye wouldn't last forever. Most of all, I knew it was a comforting sign of her amazing love for me.

Resources for Pet Loss

Downshen, Steven. "When a Pet Dies". *Kids Health*, June. 2018, www.kidshealth.org/whenapetdies.

Holloway, Sadie. "How to Talk to Children About the Death of a Pet." *Pet Helpful*, 15 July. 2019, www.pethelpful.com/howtotalktochildrenaboutthedeathofafamilypet.

Melson, Gail. "When a Pet Dies." *Why The Wild Things Are*, 14 August. 2019, www.pscyologytoday/us/blog/whythewiwildthingsare/when a pet dies.

Steven, Susan. "Talking to Kids About the Death of a Pet." *Kids Plus Pediatrics*, www.kidpluspdh.com/doctors-notes/talking-to-kids-about-the-death-of-a-pet.

Dear Readers,

I was inspired to write this book after I lost my dearest senior canine family members, Ella Rose, and Emma Rose, along with my Clydesdale, Jarisview Jodie. My past work in the veterinary field coupled with my farm life has exposed me to a plethora of animal loss, resulting in pain and insurmountable feelings of grief at times. Navigating through the gripping elements of grief is complex and certainly everyone manages grief in their own private and public ways.

As an animal advocate and enthusiast, I wanted to make a difference for individuals and families enduring this difficult time. Thus, it is my sincerest hope that this special narrative will also comfort those who have lost their beloved pet and family member. Most of all, I hope that this book demonstrates that you are never alone in the waves of goodbye.

Lastly, thank you to Alex Brown, Ted G. Fleener, Millie Godwin, Chrissy Hobbs, Kendall Knaus and Tatiana Kutsachenko for their wonderful contributions to this book. I am most grateful for their time and professional expertise.

Love & Peace,

Kristen Halverson

About the Author

Kristen Halverson lives in NE Iowa on a farm with her family. She enjoys riding horses, downhill skiing, and hiking along Lake Superior. Most of all, Kristen loves with spending time with her cherished and beloved animals. Halverson has leveraged her robust graduate education in strategic leadership with her literary missions since 2016. Her benevolence and philanthropic efforts have made a difference for horses, koalas, and the environment.

Lastly, Kristen has utilized her storybooks and picture books in public library reading programs throughout Iowa, Wisconsin, Minnesota, and Colorado. *Waves of Goodbye: A Story of Pet Loss & Comfort* is Halverson's fourteenth children's book. More information about her titles and writing services can be found at www.kristenhalversonbooks.com.

www.ingramcontent.com/pod-product-compliance
Lightning Source LLC
Chambersburg PA
CBHW042107090426

42811CB00018B/1876